Chief No Feathers' Quests

Tipi Livin'

with Silvertip Grizzly and Spirit Dog

By LMB Wordsmith
(Chief No Feathers)

Chief No Feathers' Quests

Tipi Livin'

with Silvertip Grizzly and Spirit Dog

By LMB Wordsmith
(Chief No Feathers)

<u>Table of Contents</u>

The Wolf & The Beaver 5

Watching the Swallows   (What If I Had a Million Dollars?) 14

Pointy-Side Up! – Plan B for the Middle Class...20

Silvertip Grizzly with Spirit Dog..22

About the Author (Chief No Feathers) 30

The Wolf & The Beaver

Sometime after college, with notebooks in my backpack, I went to an island in Northern Canada to create a book out of my notes.

I brought a tipi[1], about 60 days worth of food, and seeds that, according to the packages, would start to produce food in about 56 days.

____

[1] for more on tipis, see "Watching the Swallows" and "Pointy-Side Up! – Plan B for the Middle Class".

Theoretically, it was a nice plan.

Nature has a way of messing up nice plans.

First, raccoons ate all the seeds I planted. I could hear their howling in the night after each planting. Armed with a flashlight and the Winchester Model 96 rifle I had inherited from my dad, they were gone before I ever saw any. So I never got to eat any of the food I never got to grow.

Second, "60 days worth" of food was accurate **IF** I was living in a house back in town, where getting a drink of water meant turning on the faucet; cooking meant turning on the stove; and getting warm meant turning up the thermostat. It did not cover however hauling the water up in buckets from the river, nor the chopping down of trees and splitting the wood to make a fire on which to cook. And getting heat was not merely turning up the thermostat, but cutting down and hauling another tree to the campsite, splitting the wood and then carrying it into the tipi. So the "60 days worth" of food didn't last that long in the wilderness.

*****

<u>Gilligan's Island</u>

One morning I heard noises that I recognized as English words – very odd, as I knew I was alone on the island. The voices went away.

I still had enough clarity of mind then to realize that it was not my mind playing tricks with me [it would later].

Later in the morning I heard the voices again, and made my way toward the voices and down to the shore. Emerging from the brush, I came upon a man with his two teenage sons: they were dragging logs upriver to build a log cabin. With the rapids just below us, they could only drag about 4 logs at a time behind their little boat with a small motor, and they were beaching them there in front of me. The water was wide and calm upriver from me, so they could then tie them together and float-drag perhaps 12 logs at a time to their building site.

I must have been a scary sight. They thought the island was uninhabited, so were utterly surprised to see anyone, much less someone with a scraggy, unkempt 5-week old beard step out of the bushes in front of them.

Thereafter, they referred to the island as "Gilligan's Island" (after the 1960's hit comedy series by that name); and they referred to me as "Gilligan" ["Well who do you think you are, stranded on that island all by yourself?" (I had been a long distance swimmer, so had counted on that as my ace in the hole in case of any trouble)].

> [My brother had left me a small boat that could be filled and floated by blowing air into it – but the raccoons found it and punctured it all over with their teeth. Back when I was still civil toward them, I attributed their behavior as going for the salt that was in the sweat that was on the boat's skin (from when we blew it up with our own hot air).]

*****

<u>Nightline</u>

Over the next few weeks my "neighbors" would come over to visit me. They told me of a "nightline", a heavy cord one could throw out in the river with bait: then come back the next morning to find a large catfish at the end of it.

*****

<u>Don't wave a Red Flag</u>

The river was quite wide out in front of me – they lived on the other side over a mile away (a distance I once could swim quite easily). They said if I ever needed anything, to wave from the shore and they would come over. Mr. Smythe said, though, not to wave anything "red" in color – it couldn't be seen in that distance.

Several weeks later, with food running dangerously low, I went to the shore and waved my red bandana to them as a signal.

When they came by several hours later, they said they never saw the red bandana – just my green windbreaker [which I was wearing at the time while waving my red bandana] going back and forth, so they deduced I was signaling them.

*****

<u>"North" is West of here</u>

One day I was walking through the forest on the island (it was a big, long, island, perhaps a half mile wide and nearly 3 miles long). It was so far north in Canada that, while the river and island appeared on a map to be on an east-west axis, my compass read "North" as upriver to the west (the magnetic load in Western Canada [which is what compasses are attracted to] was west of me – not "north" of me).

*****

<u>The Prickly Porcupine</u>

As I was walking, I heard a distinct sound, like a rough scratching. I stopped walking, and the sound stopped. I took a couple of steps, and the sound started again. I did this several times in order to zero in on the direction of the noise. When I figured that out, I headed in that direction, stopping occasionally. By now, I realized the sound was somewhere in the air. By taking a few more steps, and looking up into the trees, I was able to see a porcupine climbing a tree, with its sharp, brittle quills, scraping the bark and making the sound.

I had left my Winchester back at the tipi, so the porcupine would win any fight we may have gotten into at that point. I also realized that if I left to get my gun, the porcupine could come back down the tree and walk away (see Mr. Smythe with the wolf [below]). So I stood under the tree and clapped. With each clap, the porcupine climbed higher. When I figured it was high enough to not have enough time to get back down in time (again, please see Mr. Smythe with the wolf below), I ran back to my tipi and got my Winchester.

I never missed with that Winchester.

> (It may also be that I never missed because I was a sharpshooter [see "The Boy Is Back!"], but I mostly put the accolades on that rifle [as Daniel Boone did with his trusty "Ol' Betsy"].)

On returning to the tree, the porcupine was still high up in it. One shot. Then with at first a slow, but then a cascading sound, the porcupine hit various branches on its way back down to hit Mother Earth with a thud.

I went to pick it up, but it got me – even if a porcupine is dead, the quills can still get you. With the barb at the end of each quill, they "stick" and stay in your hand [or your nose, if you are an inquisitive dog]. I finally figured out a way to grasp it without getting stuck by its quills.

Back at camp it was still a tricky thing to "clean" it with all the quills [and yes, I can testify that their quills constitute a very effective defense system].

After doing so, I realized that my stomach had changed so much from being without food that I couldn't eat meat anymore.[2]

---

[2] The microbes in the stomach that do the digesting of food into useful nutrition and energy change with the person's (or animal's) diet. It had changed so much by this point that I could not eat meat anymore. Even after I returned to civilization, it was still another six weeks before I could stomach eating meat again. I can now understand why people who

So I cut up the meat into bits, and used it as bait on my nightlines: I could then still eat fish. The smallest catfish I caught was over 2 feet long; a few were over 3 feet long.

*****

Fish Stories I

When the Smythe boys came over one day in their boat, I noticed a trident – a three-point spear – on the bottom of the boat.

– What's that for? I asked

~ Dad saw a big fish out here the other night when he went out checking our nightlines, so now he brings this and his gun when he goes out fishing at night.

*****

Fish Stories II

On one visit we were on the beach on the Smythe's side of the river. The Smythe kids said that some German tourists had just been there, and had asked about the fishing.

Mr. Smythe said the fishing was fine and, in fact, he had to bring a gun with him when he went out fishing.

These German tourists apparently knew enough English to say "Fish story – fish story" when Mr. Smythe told them this.

~ Well then, he said – come over and look at this, so he walked them over to his car, opened the trunk, and inside were a bunch of catfish, several well over 3 feet long!

Now they believed.

*****

Riding Bareback

On another visit, the younger Smythe kids (there were about 7 of them in total) asked if I wanted to ride a horse.

– Sure. [I had only been <u>on</u> a horse once or twice before, but had never "ridden" one.]

One of the girls went into the barn and came out with a dark brown horse. No saddle. No reins.

– How do you do it? I asked.

~ Hold onto the mane.

---

become vegetarians, whether for political, philosophical or religious reasons, can not even stomach the smells of meat cooking.

The girl brought the horse over to a fence. I climbed the fence, and from that position I mounted the horse (there were obviously no stirrups either).

Her sister, already mounted on another horse, said ~ Grab the mane.

I did.

~ Ready?

– Yep.

~ Giddy-yap!, yelled the sister, and her horse charged off and down a steep embankment.

My horse followed immediately, without any command or encouragement from me.

The sister, now travelling fast, turned around just briefly enough to shout: ~ Hold on!

I held onto the mane, somehow kept my balance, and raced bareback after her.

*****

<u>The Crane & the Blackbirds</u>

One day I was sitting on a boulder down by the river, converting my notes into a book, while the river lapped on to the shore next to me.

While writing, I heard noise out over the water.

As I honed into the sound and the direction, I saw a crane (with a wingspan well over six feet) about a mile away flying upriver.

He wasn't making the noise.

It was the 15 to 20 blackbirds that were dive-bombing him – from above, from in front, from in back, and from below – that were screeching and making the noise.

<u>Relentless dive-bombing</u>

The crane never wavered, continuing his course upriver.

The ballet – the straight and true flight of the crane and the multi-directional flights of the attacking blackbirds dive-bombing him – continued for another two or three miles . . . until the ensemble disappeared out of sight.

I returned to my writing.

*****

<u>The Immovable Object</u>

One day while walking through the forest as the effect of starvation was sinking in, I saw my path was blocked by a fallen tree. No problem, just step over it.

Next thing I knew I was on the ground looking up at the fallen tree, still blocking my path. Oh, I must not have raised my leg up far enough to make it over. No problem – I wasn't hurt and could just get up. I'll try harder raising my leg higher next time.

Several minutes later I notice that I am still lying on the ground, still looking up at the tree I failed to cross.

Well, time to get up, I thought.

Several more minutes pass, and I'm still on the ground, with not enough energy to get up. Will have to concentrate now.

After several more minutes of gathering up my energy, I was finally able to get up, climb over the log, and walk, albeit slowly, back to my tipi.

*****

<u>Wolves</u>

From time to time when I saw the Smythe's, Mr. Smythe would ask if the wolves had gotten me yet [obviously not, since I was standing in front of him, talking and joking with him], or if I had seen any wolves?

– No.

[At the time I doubted there were any wolves on the island.]

I now think there could have been wolves there at times, perhaps going over there in the winter when the river was frozen up, but not retreating toward the mainland on either side in time when the river broke up in the spring, thereby stranding them on the island for the summer.

*****

<u>Tipis</u>

Tipis are beautiful domiciles to live in.

They are actually in the form of an oval [vs. circle], with the tipi poles coming together over the <u>back center</u> of the oval. The tipi, whether made of hides or fabric, protects you from the weather and elements outside while allowing you to hear all the sounds of the forest and nature around you. (That is peaceful and pleasing to me, but I realize it may be disconcerting to others.) The fire pit is in the <u>center</u> of the oval, and the smoke exits the tipi through the tipi poles. So between the oval, the "cathedral" ceiling, the poles all pointing up toward the heavens, and the warm flickering flames of the fire, it is all quite comforting.

> [& if, by chance, some persnickety mosquitoes or other noisome insects get inside, then all you do is close the smoke flaps; build a very smoky fire; go outside and suddenly open the smoke flaps wide: out comes all the smoke and all the insects – and neither will come back in as long as the fire is kept alive and the heated air keeps rising, blocking their way back in.]

*****

<u>The Wolf & the Beaver</u>

So Mr. Smythe asks again if I have seen any wolves?

– No.

– And why do you keep asking?

~ Well, he said, because you have to be careful Gilligan, and then he related how when he was over here on the island one day, and was about to go back home for the night, he heard some noise.

He looked up and saw a wolf coming his way.

Knowing wolves can't climb trees, he quickly climbed a nearby tree to a safe height.

But the wolf stayed down below, waiting for him to come down.

He said he spent the whole night in the tree, but around dawn, the wolf walked away.

Not trusting the wolf, he stayed up in the tree in case it was just a trick.

Finally, realizing it was probably safe now, he started to climb down.

But hearing some sounds, he froze.

Looking around, he saw the wolf returning, with a beaver walking right behind him.

> *– At this point, it's a good idea to know animal behavior:*
>
> Yes, the wolf got the beaver **SO THAT** the beaver would cut the tree down **SO THAT** the wolf could get Mr. Smythe, . . . **BUT:** would a beaver really follow a wolf down a forest path?
>
> Looking straight into Mr. Smythe's eyes, I burst out laughing: **"Beautiful!"**

<u>Watching the Swallows</u>

(What If I Had a Million Dollars?)

For those without it, a common thought at times for some is what they would do if they had a million dollars.

I have faced and suffered starvation in the wilderness several times in my life.

Starvation in those circumstances is not like those of a political prisoner or civil rights activist – they can always say: ~ Aw shucks, I'm hungry, and open the refrigerator. Starvation in the wilderness occurs without the convenience of a nearby fridge.

When this was happening to me in Alaska, I sat by the fire near my tipi and wondered what I would do if I had a million dollars. I looked up into the evening sky and watched the swallows swooping and diving, catching their evening meal of insects.

Thirty years earlier I had endured starvation on an island in Northern Canada. When perchance I met some locals who were moving logs upriver and got some food[3], I danced and laughed in the forest after they left (I don't dance, and have come to laughing only late in life).

So as I watched the swallows, I wondered:

There was a Norwegian bachelor farmer from Northern Minnesota who wrote stories about his hometown, a fictional place called Lake Wobegone. He also had a Saturday afternoon radio show that was broadcast on public radio. His books were popular and best-sellers; he made his millions; and he married a girl from Scandinavia who worked with him on the radio program. After the wedding, he quit the show, and the two sailed off for Europe.

*****

Bill Gates and Warren Buffett, the two richest Americans at the time (& perhaps the two richest individuals in the world), met with students from Columbia University's Graduate School of Business in New York City [which Warren Buffett attended for one year in the early 1950's]. Questions naturally revolved around money (the school, after all, is about business, and business is foremost about making money). So several hundred eager, aggressive, driven young people asked questions about which path they should take, what they should do, to get their **First Billion Dollars** – was it computers, software, pharmaceuticals, finance, bio-technology or . . . ?

Warren Buffett's response: ***Do what interests you.***

*****

Less than a year after leaving, the former Norwegian bachelor farmer and his bride returned from Europe and he re-started his Saturday afternoon radio broadcast.

*****

There's a lead guitarist for a fabulously successful rock band from England. He was a graduate student studying Astrophysics when the rock band took off. He dropped out of (graduate) school. His thesis, which he had started, was on Solar Dust – the debris that surrounds our sun.

He toured the world with the rock band and made his millions.

In the meanwhile, the World of Astrophysics had moved away from the neighborhood and toward the Big Bang Theory and the Creation of the Universe, leaving his Solar Dust behind.

---

[3] See "The Wolf & The Beaver".

The lead singer[4] of the rock band died of AIDS, and the band[5] eventually disbanded.

With his millions, the guitarist no longer needed a fellowship to attend graduate school. He returned to school[6] and got his Ph.D. in Astrophysics with his thesis on Solar Dust. But now

---

[4] The lead singer was a Zoroastrian, a religion or belief founded by a Persian prophet which I thought no longer existed.

> [(Almost) needless to say, Zoroastrians are now persecuted – whether by Muslims or Hindus in south central Asia.]

But Zoroaster in German is "Zarathustra"

> & as you may recall, <u>Thus Spoke Zarathustra</u> was written by the PK ("Preacher's Kid") Friedrich Nietzsche [see "2 PK's"].

As for Zarathustra's Son, please see him in "On Time" in <u>On [things & stuff]</u>

> and within at: Out of nothing, nothing comes
>
> Out of No-thing, everything becomes

[5] If you listen to the lyrics of this legendary band's 3 Volume "Greatest Hits" [yes, they had that many], you will quickly recognize which lyrics came from the Zoroastrian and which came from the Astrophysicist [& which came from the explosive collaboration of the band].

[6] So the guitar player went back to school, and got a Ph.D. in Astrophysics from the Imperial College, London. He worked in his field of Astrophysics (including collaborating with NASA on a long distance space probe to Pluto) before becoming Chancellor of a college in England.

> [It is also interesting to note that one who has spent much of his academic life studying the stars [there is now an asteroid (Asteroid 52665 Brianmay) streaking through the universe named after him!], looking at <u>billions</u> of years of history [3 billion years here, 7 billion there, 20 billion over here, perhaps only a couple of million years over in that quadrant]   [and decades of his own guitar-playing life in the spotlight on every continent],
>
> *then wrote:* "Who Wants To Live Forever?"]

But he still liked to play guitar.

So besides Astrophysics and leading a college into the future, he helped re-form the old band [with some of the surviving members], adding guest artists, . . . and began touring the world and performing new music concerts in international venues.

> [I doubt this guitarist ever met Warren Buffett or the two American farmers.]

Solar Dust had become the hot topic in physics – because it is the way we search stars in distant galaxies that may have planets – planets that, like earth, may have life.[7]

*****

There's a story about two farmers who, after talking about the weather, wondered what they would do if they won the lottery and got a million dollars.

I think, said one farmer, I'd go off to all the finest fishing holes in the world – what about you?

I think, replied the other farmer, I'd continue farming until I went through that million too.

Warren Buffett is from Nebraska (he's sometimes referred to as "The Oracle from Omaha"). I don't know if the farmers ever talked to Warren, or whether Warren got his idea from the two farmers.

But I do see a difference between the old classic videos and now: his long black hair is now white – and he is **<u>smiling</u>**!

Doing what interests you is the key!

[7] BREAKING NEWS – CNN Today at 1:33 pm:

"A rocky planet found orbiting the star closest to Earth's sun is the nearest exoplanet that might have water and support life, researchers said.

"The discovery of the planet, Proxima b, has been <u>years in the making</u>. It is within the habitable zone of its star, Proxima Centauri, meaning liquid water could exist on the surface."

On the other hand, good ideas can come up independently, so maybe Warren never met either of these farmers.

*****

So as I looked up at the swallows and wondered where I would rather be and what I'd rather be doing, I realized I would be there in Alaska – but now I could afford the lumber and materials to build a cabin.

*****

Nevertheless, I still think a tipi is the best domicile to live in – except in the winter!

<u>ADDENDUM</u>

Never made the million dollars. Now realize I never will. But at least I was lucky (see "Us Gray Hairs" on luck), worked hard, saved, and was able to buy the materials for my cabin. Making a million doesn't matter anymore.

Pointy-Side Up! – Plan B for the Middle Class

There are books with titles so great [they tell the whole story in just the title] that I never – to my loss – got to read them.

One was Plan B for the Middle Class. It was about planning for a different future than the one we grew up believing we would inherit and live into.

Since I am somewhere between Plan D and Plan F, the book would no longer be a plan for the future, but a history of something lost and long in the past.

Another great book was Pointy-Side Up!, about how to construct a tipi.

But since I had already built and lived in tipis, once on an island in Northern Canada (see "The Wolf & The Beaver") and again in Alaska (see "Watching The Sparrows"), I already knew which side was "up".

*****

But the book I used (The Indian Tipi) and that still has relevance was written by a University of Nebraska professor back in the 1950's, based on his thorough and profound research of the tipi used by North American Plains Indians – complete with pictures, including tipi poles strapped to the top of his 1940's era sedan (!)

> [I'll let you read the book, but there are basically two designs: the "Cheyenne design" which was based on a 4 pole system, and the "Sioux design" which was based on a tri-pole (3 pole) design. Scouts know the inherent advantage of a tri-pole system, but 4 poles worked for the Cheyenne. (All the other poles you see sticking up into the heavens above a tipi are placed in the crooks between those 3 (or 4) poles.)]

He had details even modern Indians (that is, those in the 1950's) didn't even know about.

One was the "inside liner". Everyone knows the "outside cover" – that is the distinctive shape that everyone knows and associates with a "tipi". The "outside cover" rests on the outside of the tipi poles, but the "inside liner" is tied to the inside of the tipi poles: it serves an important function of providing insulation – both in the summer AND in the winter – to the occupants living in the tipi.

During a "Pow-Wow" in the 1950's, an old Indian woman [then in her 60's (so born sometime in the 1890's)] came inside the Professor's tipi, looked around, and said it wasn't "real".

"How so?" asked the Professor.

"This" – and she pointed to the "inside liner": "We **NEVER** had that!"

Fortunately there was an older Indian man (then in his 80's) nearby who overheard this exchange. He came over and joined the conversation: "Yes we did", he said, "but we had to leave it behind running from the cavalry."

The old Indian woman was born long after her folks had left the "inside liner" behind "running from the cavalry".

How much have we lost in our own lives (whether in terms of things, people and relationships) "running from the cavalry"?

[& for those who can appreciate this: the "cavalry" isn't always "the good guys".]

Silvertip Grizzly with Spirit Dog

Anchorage, looking eastward into the Chugach Mountains.

I saw some bear poop on a trail here in Anchorage last week, and wondered if it was black bear or grizzly bear poop. I didn't know if one could really tell the difference between bear poop. When I'm down on my land outside an old Russian village, I carry this big cartridge of pepper spray; I know other hikers who like to carry bells to warn bears of their approach. Here's how you can tell the difference between black vs. brown/grizzly bears:

> "Outdoorsmen should recognize the difference between black bear poop and grizzly bear poop. Black bear poop is smaller and contains lots of berries and squirrel fur. Grizzly bear poop smells like pepper and has little bells in it."

- Montana Fish & Game grizzly bear notice

*****

Three volcanoes, which were active at different times, could be seen from up on the observation deck. Here is one of them (while it is "sleeping").

<u>Silvertip</u>

[Preface: A well respected attorney and his wife went on a canoe trip down a northern Alaska river that emptied out into the Arctic Ocean. As they were gathering up what remained of their remains, the wildlife biologists and state troopers said the couple had done everything "right". After canoeing for miles, they landed on an island in the middle of the river and cooked supper. After properly dousing the fire and disposing of the leftovers, taking care not to bring any leftovers or cooking smells with them, they departed, canoed further, and set up camp on another island a mile or so downstream. Before crawling into their tent to go to sleep, with his hand on a pistol beneath his pillow, the attorney strung up a line around the camp site, and hung bells on it to act as a trip wire and as an alarm. Neither he nor his wife woke up alive. Grizzlies had found them in the middle of the night.]

I went to build an observation deck (which everyone else called a hunting platform) on my land near an old Russian village in Alaska. I knew there were grizzlies in the area, as well as perhaps black bear. I was told by friends and everyone else to be sure I kept a clean camp. It doesn't take a rocket scientist to figure that out – just ask any wildlife biologist.

But to my way of thinking, I didn't want to be the **ONLY** target. That just made it too easy for the grizzlies.

So I threw empty tin cans all around, particularly on all trails leading toward my tent (before I could perch it up on the observation deck). The idea being I'd have some warning (possibly) before a massive claw came slashing through the tent wall.

My tent – My fortress and protection against grizzlies.

Alaska Fireweed, the prettiest "weed" I know of, surrounds my fortress, adding an extra circle of protection.

One weekend my ex-mother-in-law and her new husband invited me to join some bikers on their annual weekend at Hope, an old village in Alaska where one of the early discoveries of gold occurred over a century earlier.

It was in August, when the salmon were coming in. Salmon are one of those strange fish that start life in fresh water, then go out to sea and salt water for several years, and then return to fresh water. It is NOT true that they ALL return to the same stream they came from. If such were true, they could be wiped out. Most do, perhaps 97% or so, but not all. The ones that don't are called pioneers (also see "When Times Were Bad" and "Another Day On The Yukon" for more regarding pioneers). And it is the pioneers who allow the species to have an escape hatch, an alternative, if something goes wrong with the original stream.

But with salmon come grizzlies.

Nothing went amiss, though federal and state authorities had enough posters out to warn people about their behavior and the presence of bears.

On my way back to my land, I wondered how my camp would appear. I had seen bear poop within 100 yards of my tent, and moose running through at night missed my head by a mere 18 inches.

So it was with some apprehension that I parked my truck, donned my backpack, and hiked back in to my camp.

When I got there I was relieved to find it had been untouched [and the maid hadn't come by to clean up either].

I dropped my backpack, and went back to the truck to get some more supplies.

When you break out of the woods going back to the truck, the trail leads down to a creek, crosses it, and then up the other side, through some alders, up a moose trail and then to an open area before it comes out to where I had parked my truck.

But after crossing and coming up from the creek, as I emerged from the alders, I looked up – and there, staring at me, was a grizzly bear about 35 feet away.

> *A week earlier, about 50 miles north of where I was standing, a man had gone out walking with his dog. Grizzlies and dogs don't mix. In fact, grizzlies don't seem to mix with anything else – including other grizzlies. The man and his dog came upon a grizzly. He said he first saw it about 90 feet away when it charged him. He had a pistol. As he backpedaled as fast as he could, he said he got off some wild shots. The grizzly kept coming. He was lucky, he said – one of the wild shots got the grizzly just right, so when it crashed into his leg, all he got was a bruise. The grizzly was dead.*

So this is in my mind when I see this grizzly 35 feet up the trail. Yes, the trail is a moose trail. Yes, the grizzly's nose was within 2 feet of the moose trail. Yes, the grizzly was in the right spot for its next meal.

But I don't carry a pistol. I didn't have a gun. I only had a can of pepper spray on my belt.

When I saw the grizzly[8], I froze. As it stared back at me, I slowly moved my hand to the pepper spray and unhooked it from my belt. I put my finger on the safety, and released it.

---

[8] The grizzlies in the Talkeetna Mountains between Palmer and Glennallen Alaska are an interesting bunch: when they hear a gunshot, they do not run away – instead, they run TOWARD the gunshot! They have learned that a gunshot means some hunter has just killed [or at least shot at] a moose.

So like buzzards in the South, they come running for a free meal [courtesy of some ignorant hunter].

One hunter learned this the hard way – he was just lucky his horse was faster than that particular grizzly.

I saw this Silvertip Grizzly about 35 feet away – well within the danger zone: A photographer up at Denali saw a grizzly about 150 feet away and started taking

The Montana Fish & Game warning came to mind. I figured if the grizzly charged, I would wait till it was about 10 feet away when I would pull an old football move – fake one way and then jump another way, while firing the pepper spray.

I figured the fake and maneuver would give me an extra half second. A half second for the pepper spray to act, and the bear, hopefully, to flee. Sometimes, a half second is all you get or can hope for[9] (and was certainly more than the attorney and his wife got up on that Northern Alaskan river).

It seemed close to 20 to 30 seconds while the grizzly and I stared at each other. She was the most beautiful bear I had ever seen. She was silver, a color I did not know in association with grizzlies. In Juneau, I had seen a cinnamon bear [yes, it was dead, stuffed, in an exhibit at the Juneau airport]. In Terrace, British Columbia, I had learned of the Kermode, a white bear that wasn't a polar bear [it's a black bear, but because it has a mutant gene for hair color . . . it is white]. But I had never heard of a silver bear [I learned years later it is called a Silvertip].

Besides being the most beautiful bear I had ever seen, she was also the healthiest looking bear I had ever seen.

Then with a **HUFF!, a violent, loud and startling sound**, she got up, turned around, and tore off through the forest behind her.

Yes, bears are as fast as they say; they are as powerful as they say; **but what they don't say** is that when you **mix adrenaline with that mass and power**, they are nearly unstoppable

> *[remember, it took 25 high caliber bullets from 5 park rangers and state troopers to bring down the grizzly that ate Tim the Bear Man and his girlfriend near McNeil River[10]].*

Fortunately, this Silvertip took off. And because she did, we both got to live another day.

[Please see Moe and Werner Heisenberg on this very point in "When Times Were Bad".]

Spirit Dog

I don't really believe in Spirit Dogs, but have no other way to account for what happened here:

About a week after my encounter with the grizzly, I was returning to my camp from town and headed down the trail toward the alders from which I had emerged when I first saw the Silvertip. I use a lot of senses when I'm out walking in the wilds. I heard something and

---

photographs. The grizzly noticed him and started charging the photographer. He raced the 150 feet between them and attacked and killed the photographer.

   Denali Park Rangers who found the photographer's mauled corpse figured out later what had happened by viewing the pictures in the photographer's camera.

[9] Also see "Man On Fire".

[10] For more on grizzly bears around McNeil River, see "Samoan".

stopped short. I was standing about 2 feet from where the grizzly's nose had been a week earlier. The noise was approaching, coming up the trail and through the alders. There's absolutely no reason to believe that just because I was lucky once with a grizzly that I'd ever be lucky again.

I waited, and an animal emerged from the alders: But instead of being a grizzly, it was a beautiful dog, perhaps a Border Collie. Dogs and I do get along. [Yet see "Just Tryin' To Do My Job, Ma'am" for an exception.] So I started to walk down the trail while she walked up it. I put my hand out for her to smell it (which she did), and then we passed each other and continued on our respective ways.

I went through the alders, down to the creek, crossed it, and went up the other side of the valley. For whatever reason, I decided to look back. The Border Collie had apparently changed her mind, turned around, and was now on my side of the alders. As I looked, she walked down to the creek, crossed it, and came up to me. We both walked back to my camp.

I wondered if it might be hungry, so offered it some food but she didn't take it. She just laid down by the portal to my tent (see picture of tent and Alaska Fireweed above).

This was the first night I had finished enough work to be able to sleep on my observation deck.

The last time I saw her (it doesn't get dark at night at that time of the year in that area of Alaska), she was laying next to my tent. It seemed like she was there just to protect me from any danger that comes with that territory. The next morning, when I looked down at my tent, she was gone, and I never saw her again.

Three volcanoes (active at different times) as well as moose and grizzlies could be seen from up on the observation deck.

[I used a light load utility grade ladder to get up on the observation deck – in case a grizzly (or black) bear decided to climb up it to get me, the ladder would break and collapse. (Then I would just have to wait it out like Mr. Smythe did with the wolf – see "The Wolf & The Beaver".)]

<u>Talking with the neighbors</u>

From talking with my neighbors there, I learned that the silver bear denned near another neighbor's house. They knew her, and she knew them. My neighbors knew me, and I knew my neighbors. It's just that the Silvertip and I didn't know each other.

Not Again!

Several months later I'm back in Juneau and it actually started getting dark at night again.

One evening I was outside my apartment charging up an old truck battery while standing under a bright light.

I hear a noise, a clicking sound, down the driveway and look. But I couldn't see anything.

I turn my attention back to the battery.

I hear the clicking sound again – I look.

It's a black bear, about 25 feet away.

I think: I'm tired of this.

I say: What do you want?

It doesn't answer me.

I say again, in a deeper, gruffer voice: What do you want?

It still doesn't answer me, but then I see that it is walking down the driveway away from me, and I can hear the clicking of its toenails on the pavement.

But for whatever reason, I didn't trust this black bear. I went upstairs to my neighbor. I knew she had a pistol. I also knew she had been a diesel mechanic in the US Navy; that she was in security; and that she had tackled a prospective thief at the store she was guarding. In short, she was tough.

We came back down and stood on the porch with the pistol. While the driveway where I was working and had seen the bear was to our right, we heard noise to our left and looked.

There, peeking around the corner, was the black bear. After leaving me and going back down the driveway, it had circled back and around our apartment building.

My neighbor looked at her. ~ Yeah, she says, she's the same one she had seen at a friend's house several blocks away a couple of weeks earlier.

The bear turned, walked through another neighbor's yard, and then out to the street where she walked away.

My neighbor went back upstairs with her pistol, and I went back to finish charging the battery.

<u>About the Author (Chief No Feathers)</u>

Chief No Feathers & His Loyal Scout Muddy Paws

At the end of the Indian Wars out West, photographers from the East went out to photograph a disappearing way of life, if not quite a disappearing people.

[I have always known this photograph existed –

I had just never seen it before now.]

Sioux encampment[11]

---

[11] Can you tell which way the prevailing wind is blowing?

I saw this with seagulls in a parking lot in Delaware over a century later (except the seagulls were facing *into* the wind).

The Sioux have their smoke flaps set so that the smoke from the fires within their tipis (to keep them warm and to cook their food), [and so that the drafts for those fires are better and stronger] . . . blows away from their camp.

The "savages" at least knew what they were doing.

Some of the photographers concentrated on the people, their tipis and their camps, while others concentrated on taking portraits of their chiefs.

One of these portraits was of Chief Two Feathers.

I have no idea who Chief Two Feathers was, what his claim to fame might have been, or how he might have earned the two feathers. All I know is that there is a photograph of him.

*****

While working for the Tribe at the Fort, I was severely injured, with the injury requiring major surgery. When I went back about a week later to have the stitches removed from the various incisions, I was talking to the assistant surgeon. He asked what I did. I said I was the Executive Director of a tribe, but I didn't know if I was the Chief non-chief, or a non-chief Chief.

The surgeon, earlier in his career, like many doctors in Alaska, had worked out in the Bush in various villages, and knew of the tenuous and fluctuating reality of tribal power. I told him that while the staff and tribal members preferred to call me "Boss" (their term – not a term of my choosing), that there were real, but unspoken, limits to my authority.

~ Oh, said the surgeon, so you're like a chief with no feathers.

— Exactly – Chief No Feathers!

*****

Little Miss Bella has just put her right front paw on Captain Sparky's back,
so he is about to react. (Blue huckleberries can be seen growing behind Sparky's tail.)

Golden colored fish can be seen in the pond behind the puppies.
[They were all subsequently wiped out by being eaten by Snapping Turtles
(see "The Prehistoric Creature With The Dinosaur Tail").]

I had several projects going on at the Lower Pond, including building a dam to raise the water level of the pond, and a deck (see above) so we could go out over the pond and look down at the fish swimming by below. Captain Sparky and Little Miss Bella would be out there with me while I worked and they played. Shih Tzu's are not water dogs like Spaniels, so do not go out to swim. But they do recognize water for the purposes of drinking, and freely did so. While Little Miss Bella could do so without getting all messy, Sparky had a way of always finding the mud – hence his well-earned nickname: "Muddy Paws".

So when it was time for a break, and we'd go out to explore the forest, it was Chief No Feathers and his loyal scout Muddy Paws who went out with Little Miss Bella to see what the forest had in store for us that day.